MR DOO

BALLOON SCIENCE

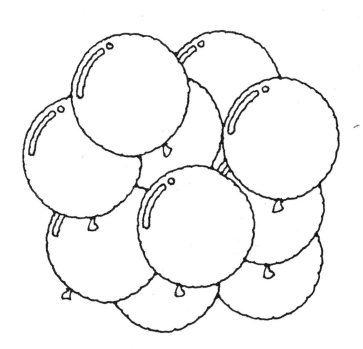

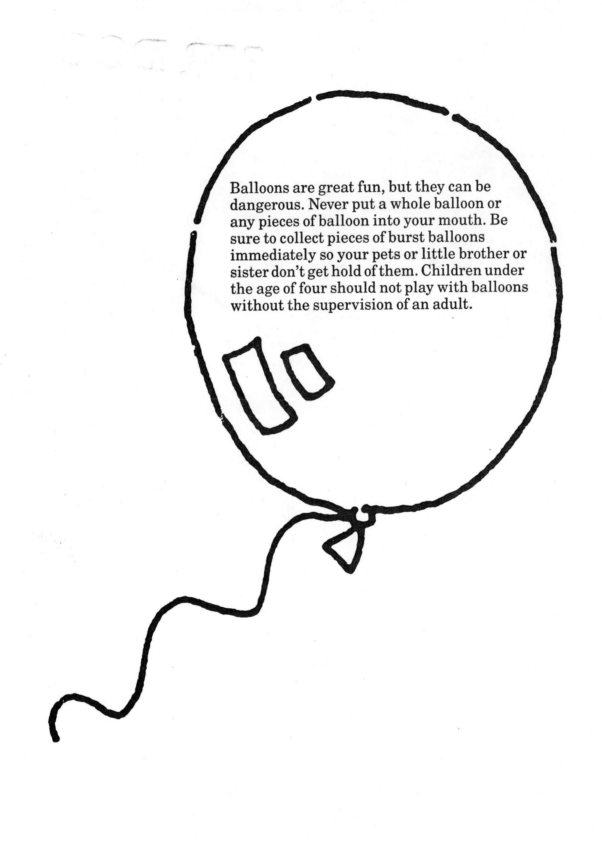

Balloons are great fun, but they can be dangerous. Never put a whole balloon or any pieces of balloon into your mouth. Be sure to collect pieces of burst balloons immediately so your pets or little brother or sister don't get hold of them. Children under the age of four should not play with balloons without the supervision of an adult.

BALLOON SCIENCE

Written by Etta Kaner
Illustrated by Louise Phillips

ADDISON-WESLEY PUBLISHING COMPANY, INC.

Reading, Massachusetts   Menlo Park, California   New York
Don Mills, Ontario   Wokingham, England   Amsterdam   Bonn
Sydney   Singapore   Tokyo   Madrid   San Juan

Library of Congress Cataloging-in-Publication Data

Kaner, Etta.
    Balloon science / written by Etta Kaner ; illustrated by Louise Phillips.
        p.   cm.
        Summary: Presents a collection of balloon experiments, activities, games, riddles, and surprising facts.
        ISBN 0-201-52378-7
        1. Balloons—Experiments—Juvenile literature.   2. Air—Experiments—Juvenile literature.   3. Science—Experiments—Juvenile literature.   [1. Balloons—Experiments.   2. Experiments.] I. Phillips, Louise, ill.   II. Title.
    QC33.K36   1989
    530'.078—dc20   90-33873
                                                                  CIP
                                                                  AC

First published in Canada by Kids Can Press, Ltd., 585½ Bloor Street West, Toronto, Ontario, Canada M6G 1K5.

Edited by Laurie Wark
Book design by Tony Delitala
Cover illustration by Fred Harsh
Set in 11-point Century Schoolbook by
Compeer Typographic Services

1 2 3 4 5 6 7 8 9–BA–96959493
First printing, April 1993

CONTENTS

Introduction   8

Amazing Air   **10**
Weighing Air   12
Hold on Tight   14
How Do You Breathe?   16
Where's the Low Pressure?   18
Take a Balloon for a Walk   20
Do Balloons Share?   22
Popping Ears   24
The Escaping Air Mystery   26

Put Air to Work   **28**
Air Power   30
Air that Sticks Like Glue   32
Test Your Strength   34
Balloon Blast-off   36
Look Ma, No Hands   38
Which is Stronger
  —You or Air?   40

Water Works   **42**
An Underwater Diver   44
Water Flowing Uphill   46
The Balloon-motor Boat Race   48
Sink a Submarine   50
Build a Hovercraft   52
A Land Floater   54

**Helium and
Hot Air High Jinks**   **56**
How to Stop a Blimp
  From Escaping   58
A New Pet—The Flouncer   60
Warm Air vs. Cold Air   62
Get a Rise Out of Air   64
Create a Vacuum   66

Charge It   **68**
Angry Balloons   70
Snap, Crackle and Hop   72
Lightning Without a Rainstorm   74
A Magnetic Balloon   76
An Unusual Flashlight   78
No Strings Attached   80
A Magical Merry-go-round   82

**Be A Carbon Dioxide
Detective**   **84**
Get the Inside Story   86
The Baking Powder Challenge   87
The Pop Contest   88
Eating Carbon Dioxide   90

What Comes First?   92
The End of the Beginning   94
Index   96

Acknowledgements

I would like to thank the following people for their generous assistance in the production of this book: Claire Mackay, for her encouragement and for getting me on the right track. Sheila Freedman, Leigh Turina, John Varga and the Pioneer Balloon Co. for their enthusiastic supply of resource materials. John Fowles and Mel Dwosh, for their patient scientific explanations. Marilyn Cooney of Balloonman of Canada and Hugh Wallace and Flora MacDonald, co-owners of Cameron Balloons Ontario, for revealing the amazing world of balloons to me. The staff at Kids Can Press, especially Val Wyatt and Laurie Wark, for their enthusiasm and high degree of professionalism. The employees of countless manufacturers, for their cheerful explanations of "how it works." My dear family, for putting up with my experiments and balloon riddles.

For Yael, Ora and David

INTRODUCTION

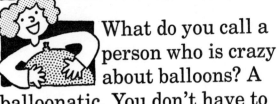

What do you call a person who is crazy about balloons? A balloonatic. You don't have to be a balloonatic to enjoy this book. You just have to be curious about how things work. After you do each experiment, expand your curiosity by trying the What happens if section. I'm sure you'll be able to think of your own what ifs

★ **THIS WAY FOR FUN • FACTS • EXPERIMENTS • JOKE**

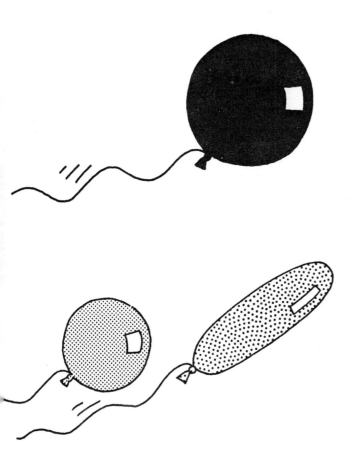

too. In addition to balloon experiments, you'll find oodles of surprising facts, creative fun and games. You'll also find some loony riddles like this one:

Q: What do a balloon and a fairy have in common?

A: They both have air in them (f-air-y).

You'll need plenty of air to do all of the activities in *Balloon Science.* Take a deep breath and have a balloon, I mean, ball.

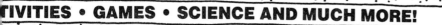

AMAZING AIR

What's strong enough to hold up an airplane
yet small enough to sneak through a balloon? It's air.
Find out how air can do these stunts and others
when you do these experiments.

Weighing Air

Hold out your hand, palm up. The air you're
holding weighs about 45 kilograms (100 pounds).
That's a lot more than you weigh.
If you don't believe that air has weight, try this
experiment and find out.

You'll need:
- ○ *2 straight pins*
- ○ *1 straw*
- ○ *2 identical balloons*
- ○ *1 piece of yarn 30 cm
  (1 foot) long*
- ○ *tape*

1. Push the pins all the
way through the straw
so that each pin is 1 cm (½
inch) from either end of the
straw.

2. Attach the deflated
balloons to the pins by
sticking the pins through
the rubber just below the
balloons' rings.

3. Tie one end of the
yarn at the middle of the
straw. Tie the other end to
a place where it can hang
freely.

4. Move the yarn slowly
along the straw until it
balances. Put a small piece
of tape on the yarn so that
it doesn't move.

5. Remove the balloons
from the pins.

6. Inflate one balloon
fully and tie it. Inflate the
other balloon to half the
size of the first.

7. Put the balloons back
onto the pins. What
happens?

How does it work?

The straw becomes unbalanced because the larger balloon is heavier than the smaller balloon. It is heavier because the air inside the larger balloon weighs more. Are you surprised that air has weight? At sea level, the air in a box the size of two school desks weighs 1 kilogram (about 2 pounds). That's about as heavy as five large oranges. It looks like air isn't such a light-weight after all.

What happens if . . .

● you inflate both balloons to the same size?
● you inflate one balloon to one-quarter the size of the other?

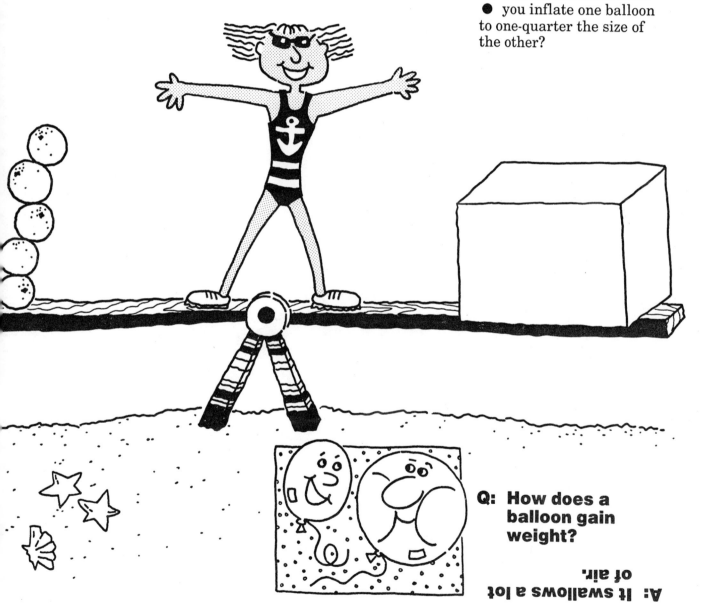

Q: How does a balloon gain weight?

A: It swallows a lot of air.

Hold On Tight

How would you get cups to stick to an inflated
balloon using water instead of glue?
Amaze yourself and your friends when you find
out how it's done.

You'll need:
- ○ *a balloon*
- ○ *2 plastic cups*
- ○ *a sink*
- ○ *an empty bowl*

1. Inflate the balloon to half its fully-inflated size and tie it.

2. Fill both cups with very hot tap water. Let them stand so that the plastic will heat up.

3. In the meantime, fill the sink with ice cold water.

4. Now work quickly. Empty the hot water into the bowl. Press the mouths of the cups against the sides of the balloon. As you hold the cups against the balloon, dip them one after another into the cold water until they cool off.

5. Let go of the cups. What happens?

 ## How does it work?

When the hot cups are cooled, the cooled air inside them contracts and takes up less space. There is now more room for part of the balloon to be pushed into the cup by the air pressure inside the balloon. The balloon holds on by pressing against the insides of the cups.

In the past, doctors heated small glass cups over a flame and pressed them against the skin of a patient to help cure bronchitis and asthma. As the air cooled the cups, the skin was sucked up into the cup. This increased the flow of blood under the skin. They called this "cupping." Today some doctors use cupping to help people with rheumatism.

What happens if . . .

● you try to remove the cups without touching them? Hint: try hot water or a pencil.

How Old Can a Balloon Get?

Balloons will last for years if they are kept under the right conditions. The best place to keep a package of balloons is in a cool, dry, dark place. Heat makes rubber gooey, extreme cold makes it brittle, and sunlight can change its colour. Leave a white balloon on a window sill that has a lot of sunshine. After a month, you'll have a pink balloon.

Q: What do balloons eat at picnics?

A: Ballooney sandwiches.

15

How Do You Breathe?

Doctors take an X-ray of your lungs to see if the lungs are healthy. But X-rays are just pictures. You can get a better idea of how your lungs work by making a moving model of one of them.

You'll need:
- *a 1-L (1-quart) empty clear plastic bottle— a cooking oil bottle is ideal*
- *a serrated knife*
- *2 balloons, one large and one small*
- *2 rubber bands*
- *1 straw*
- *some Plasticine or other modelling clay*

1. With a grown-up's help, cut off the bottom of the bottle with a serrated knife.

2. Cut the neck off the large balloon and stretch it over the bottom of the bottle. Put a rubber band around it to hold it in place.

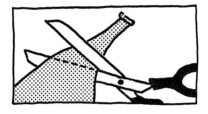

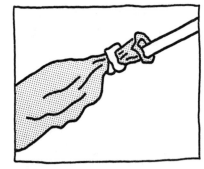

3. Insert the straw into the neck of the other balloon. Tie the balloon to the straw with the other rubber band.

4. Put the balloon and part of the straw into the bottle. Hold the straw in place by wrapping a blob of Plasticine around it. Make sure the Plasticine completely covers the mouth of the bottle.

5. Push up on the rubber at the bottom of the bottle. What happens? Is this like breathing in or out?

6. Pull the rubber down. Which way would you be breathing now?

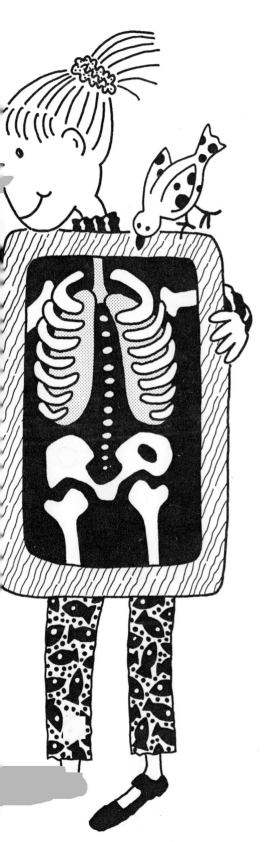

How does it work?

The stretched balloon works like the flat muscle at the bottom of your chest cavity. This muscle is called a diaphragm. The diaphragm forces air in and out of your lungs. When the diaphragm goes up, the greater air pressure in the bottle (chest cavity) pushes on the balloon (lung). The air is pushed out of the balloon (lung) and up the straw which is your airway. You are exhaling or breathing out. When the diaphragm goes down, there is less pressure in the bottle (chest cavity). Air is sucked into the balloon (lung) through the straw (airway). You are inhaling or breathing in.

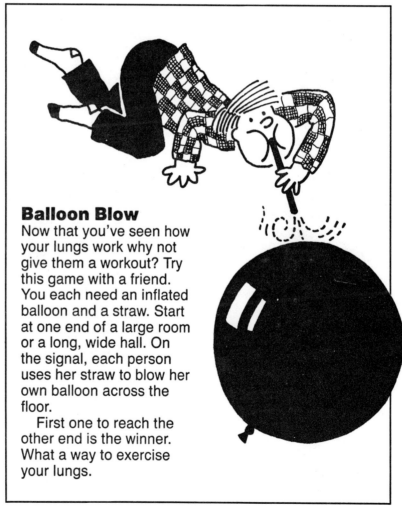

Balloon Blow

Now that you've seen how your lungs work why not give them a workout? Try this game with a friend. You each need an inflated balloon and a straw. Start at one end of a large room or a long, wide hall. On the signal, each person uses her straw to blow her own balloon across the floor.

First one to reach the other end is the winner. What a way to exercise your lungs.

Where's the Low Pressure?

Have you ever wondered how a heavy airplane can be supported by air? In part, its because high and low pressure work together to produce an upward push called lift. You don't need to fly to see how this works. You just need a little lung power.

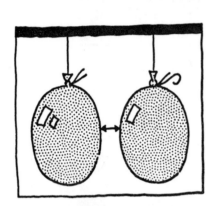

You'll need:
- *two balloons inflated to the same size*
- *two pieces of string about 30 cm (12 inches) long*

1. Use the string to hang the balloons so that there is 3 cm (1¼ inches) between them.

2. Blow gently between the balloons.

3. Don't be surprised if you can't blow them apart. As a matter of fact, they'll come closer together.

How does it work?

Almost two hundred years ago, a Swiss scientist named Daniel Bernoulli discovered that fast-moving air has low pressure. When you blew the air between the balloons you made it move faster and created low pressure in that area. The stiller air on the sides of the balloons had greater pressure than the moving air. This higher pressure air forced the balloons together.

Prison Break-out

If you were locked in a prison with only a balloon, how would you get out? Assassin bugs would have no problem. When their babies are ready to hatch out of the egg, a kind of balloon inside the egg fills up with gas until it bursts. The force of the exploding balloon breaks open the egg and the bug escapes.

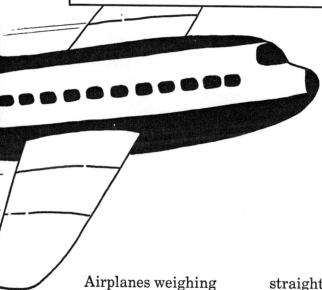

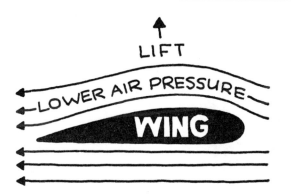

Airplanes weighing several tons can fly because of this difference in air pressure. Look at an airplane's wing from the side. It's curved on top and flat at the bottom. When a plane moves forward air rushes over and under its wings. The air flowing over the curve must move more quickly to reach the end of the wing at the same time as the air moving in a straight line underneath. This creates a lower pressure above the wing. The higher pressure under the wing can lift up the airplane. This upward push of high air pressure is called lift.

What happens if . . .
● you blow harder between the balloons?
● you blow at the side of one of the balloons?

Q: Why did the balloon stow away on the airplane?

A: It needed a lift.

Take a Balloon for a Walk

Challenge a friend to make a balloon "walk" through the air without her touching it. After she has tried a few times and failed, show her how.

What a lot of hot air!

You'll need:
- ○ *an inflated balloon*
- ○ *a hair blower*

1. Set the hair blower at low speed and cool air. Turn it on.

2. Point the nozzle straight upward and hold the balloon above it for a moment. Once the balloon is caught in the air stream, let it go. Slowly walk forward with the blower. If you use an extension cord, you can take the balloon for a walk across the room and back without touching it.

How does it work?

Why doesn't the balloon move away from the stream of air? Remember Bernoulli's discovery? (See page 18.) Slow-moving air has greater pressure than fast-moving air. So, if the balloon moves to one side of the fast-moving airstream, the slow-moving air surrounding it pushes the balloon back. This keeps the balloon directly over the blower.

What happens if . . .
● you turn the blower to high speed?
● you raise or lower the blower?

Footballoon

Another way to keep a balloon in the air is by tossing it with your foot. How long can you and your friends keep a balloon up in the air using only your feet? Either use one balloon and make it a group challenge by counting the total number of tosses, or give each person his own balloon.

On the signal, each person counts how many times he can kick the balloon before it touches the floor. Remember: only feet may be used.

Do Balloons Share?

What would happen if two balloons of different sizes had to share the same air? Set up your experiment and predict what will happen. You'll be surprised at the actual results.

You'll need:
- O *2 identical balloons*
- O *2 clothespins*
- O *a spool of thread with a single hole through it*

1. Inflate one of the balloons almost completely.

2. Twist the balloon's neck and clamp it with a clothespin so that no air escapes.

3. Put the open part of the neck over one end of the spool.

4. Inflate the second balloon to one-quarter the size of the first one. Clamp it with the second clothespin and put its neck over the other end of the spool.

5. Remove both clothespins at the same time. Do the balloons share the air?

How does it work?

Why does air flow from the small balloon to the bigger balloon? Because there's more pressure in the smaller balloon. You can see this for yourself when you try to blow up a balloon. It takes a lot more lung power (air pressure) to blow into the balloon when it's small than it does when it's bigger and more stretched.

This experiment works the same way. The greater air pressure in the small balloon forces the air into the larger balloon.

This principle is used by the gas company to deliver gas to our homes from thousands of kilometres (miles) away. After gas is pumped up from underground, it is put under high pressure. It flows along the pipelines to your home where the pressure is much lower.

What happens if . . .
● you inflate the second balloon to half the size of the first one?
● you inflate both balloons the same amount?

It's a Bird, It's a Plane, It's Superballoon!

Meteorologists send huge six-metre (yard) wide balloons into the upper atmosphere twice a day. Each of these hydrogen filled balloons carries equipment that measures air pressure, temperature and humidity (moisture) of the air. They also have a small radio transmitter which sends information to a weather station on the ground. As the balloon gets higher into the atmosphere the air pressure decreases. The greater pressure inside the balloon pushes outward just as if someone were still blowing it up. After about one and a half hours, the balloon can't stretch any more. It bursts and the equipment parachutes safely to the earth.

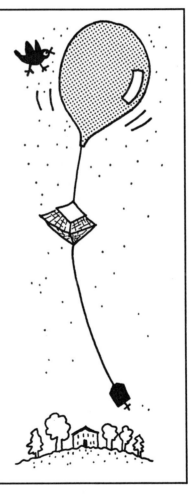

23

Popping Ears

Do your ears pop when you go up rapidly in a high-rise elevator or when you take off in an airplane? This P-O-P happens when there's a sudden change in air pressure. Here's an experiment that shows how your eardrums react when air pressure changes.

You'll need:
- ○ *a balloon*
- ○ *scissors*
- ○ *an empty pill bottle without a lid*
- ○ *an empty 1-L (1-quart) jar with a wide mouth*
- ○ *a ball of Plasticine or other modelling clay the size of a small tomato*
- ○ *a vacuum cleaner*

1. Cut the balloon in half across its width.

2. Stretch the top half of the balloon over the mouth of the pill bottle so that the rubber is taut.

3. Stand the pill bottle on the bottom of the jar.

4. Flatten the Plasticine to make a lid for the jar.

5. Make a hole through the centre of the Plasticine lid. Fit the end of the vacuum cleaner nozzle through the hole and press the Plasticine around the nozzle to eliminate any air holes.

6. Tightly cover the jar with the lid and hose. The hose should be near the top of the jar.

7. Turn on the vacuum cleaner.

How does it work?

When the vacuum cleaner sucks air out of the jar, there is less air pressure pushing down on the balloon. This allows the greater air pressure inside the pill bottle to push the balloon outwards. The balloon is like your eardrum. When you are on the ground the air pressure on both sides of your eardrum is the same. There is less air pressure the higher you go. In a rapidly ascending elevator or airplane, the air pressure on the outside of your eardrum suddenly becomes less than the pressure on the inside. Greater air pressure on the inside of your eardrum causes it to bulge outwards. Swallowing releases this inside pressure since it forces air away from your eardrum toward your throat.

What happens if . . .
● you use a larger jar?
● you change the size of the pill bottle?

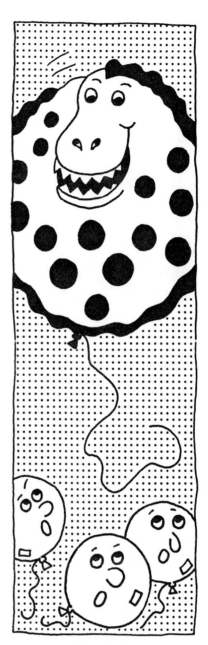

READY?

Q: What do you call a giant balloon that eats other balloons?

A: A Balloonosaurus Rex.

25

The Escaping Air Mystery

Have you ever wondered why your balloons shrink a few days after your birthday party? How does the air escape? Here's a way to solve this mystery.

You'll need:
- *a funnel*
- *a few balloons*
- *vanilla extract*
- *soya sauce*
- *lemon juice*

1. Use the funnel to put a few drops of vanilla extract into a balloon. Inflate and tie it.

2. After ten minutes smell the outside of the balloon. What happened?

3. Do the same with the soya sauce and the lemon juice in separate balloons. Do you have to wait ten minutes before you can smell them?

How does it work?

All things are made up of tiny particles called molecules. Since you could smell the vanilla, soya sauce and lemon juice, their molecules must be small enough to sneak between the larger rubber balloon molecules. Rubber has giant molecules. Just as a jar of large marbles has bigger spaces than a jar of small marbles, so rubber molecules have large spaces between them. The air molecules inside your birthday balloons are also small enough to escape between the rubber molecules.

26

Don't Waste Your Breath

Are you having trouble blowing up a balloon? Stretch it a few times. Now try it. It's a snap, right? Why?

Balloons are made up of rubber molecules which are connected by string-like bonds. When you stretch the molecules in the balloon, some of the bonds break. When you let go, the molecules return to their original position, but the bonds remain broken. This makes the balloon more flexible and easier to blow up.

Instant Heat

Hold an uninflated balloon against your upper lip and stretch it quickly. Do you feel a change in the temperature of the balloon? The moving molecules generate heat.

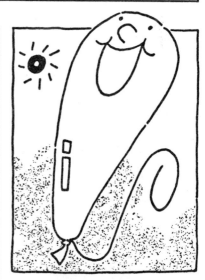

Q: What is the first thing a balloon does when it wakes up in the morning?

A: It stretches.

27

PUT AIR TO WORK

If you need a heavy-duty job done call on air. Find out how air is used to: propel hovercraft, break up concrete roads and do other amazing feats of strength.

Air Power

What is invisible and yet has the power to break up concrete roads or lift up a pile of books? Believe it or not, it's air. Try this experiment and you'll see it happen before your very eyes.

You'll need:
- *a balloon that's been stretched a few times*
- *a heavy book*

1. Lay the balloon on a table so that its neck is hanging over the edge of the table.

2. Put the book on top of the balloon.

3. Take a deep breath and blow into the balloon. Can you blow long enough to make the book flip over?

An Inflatable Invitation

The next time you have a party, send your friends an invitation that will give them a lift. Inflate a balloon and close it with a clothespin. With a permanent marker, write the time, date, place and reason for the party. Let out the air and mail your balloon invitation. This is one time your friends won't complain about inflation.

How does it work?

When you blow into the balloon, you raise the air pressure inside it. This pressure is strong enough to lift up the book.

A pneumatic hammer uses compressed air to break up concrete roads. Air pressure inside the machine forces a piston to push down firmly on a drill. The force is strong enough to shatter concrete.

What happens if . . .

● you use more books?
● you use a larger balloon?

Q: Why did the balloon quit its job at the air pump shop?

A: It couldn't stand the pressure.

31

Air that Sticks Like Glue

If you wanted to get to the top of a high tower, how would you do it? Would you take an elevator? climb the stairs? or use suction cups? Daniel Goodwin, also known as the Spider Man, climbed up the outside of a 440-m (1454-foot) tower using only suction cups. How is that possible? Try this experiment to find out.

You'll need:
- *a balloon*
- *a plastic cup with a smooth rim*

1. Inflate the balloon about one-third of its fully inflated size but don't tie it.

2. Hold the mouth of the cup against the end of the balloon. Continue blowing until the balloon is twice as big as before.

3. While you hold the balloon closed, let go of the cup. What happens?

How does it work?

As you blow, the curve of the balloon flattens and there is less balloon inside the cup. This creates more room for the air inside the cup so the air spreads out. When the air spreads out it exerts less pressure. Now there is more air pressure outside the cup than inside. The greater outside air pressure pushes the cup against the balloon and makes it stick like glue.

Suction cups that work the same way are used for carrying large panes of glass. Two rubber cups, attached to either end of a metal handle, are placed

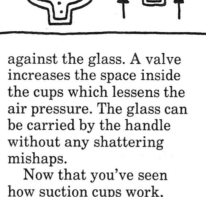

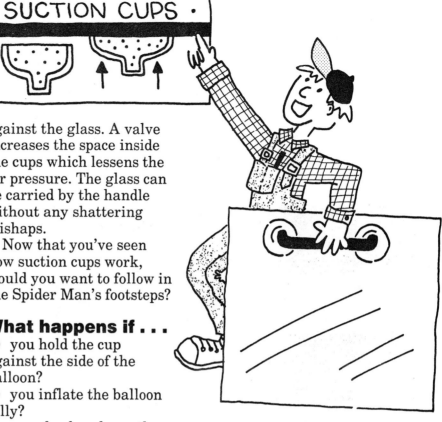

against the glass. A valve increases the space inside the cups which lessens the air pressure. The glass can be carried by the handle without any shattering mishaps.

Now that you've seen how suction cups work, would you want to follow in the Spider Man's footsteps?

What happens if . . .
● you hold the cup against the side of the balloon?
● you inflate the balloon fully?
● you slowly release the air?

The Balloon Without a Bang

Tell a friend that your inflated balloon has lost its bang. To prove it, slowly stick a pin into the end of the balloon. Your friend will be surprised and puzzled when the balloon doesn't pop.

There is less inside air pressure pushing against the end of the balloon than against its sides. In addition, the elasticity of the rubber makes it bounce back to close up the hole.

Test
Your Strength

Do you think you're strong enough to burst
a balloon with your bare hands? Here's a challenge
for anyone who thinks they have muscle power.

Hey, let me try!

You'll need:
○ *an inflated balloon*
○ *a book as large as the balloon*

1. Lay the balloon on a table.

2. Place the book on top of the balloon. Press down with your hands as hard as you can. Why is it so difficult to burst the balloon?

How does it work?

When you pressed on the book, the force that you put on the balloon was spread out over the whole balloon. That's why the balloon was able to support your weight.

Hovercraft work in the same way. Hovercraft are boats that look like rectangular flying saucers. They travel over water or on land on a cushion of air that makes the boat hover just above the surface. The cushion of air, from fans blowing downward, can support dozens of cars and as many as 400 passengers because their weight is distributed over the whole air cushion. Propellers on the top of the boat move it forward.

What happens if . . .
● you put the balloon and book on the floor and you use your body weight?
● you use a larger balloon?
● you inflate the balloon less?

Does a Balloon Eraser Work?
If balloons are made of rubber and erasers are made of rubber, can you rub out a pencil mark with a balloon? Try it.

The balloon doesn't work because its surface is too smooth. An eraser has tiny hard pieces of rubber that scratch the surface of the paper and erase the pencil mark. What about a rubber band? Would it make a good eraser?

Q: Why should you never tell a balloon a joke?

A: It might burst out laughing.

35

Balloon Blast-off

By putting air to work you can make a balloon
rocket blast through space.

You'll need:
- *thin string or thread*
- *a straw*
- *a chair*
- *tape*
- *a long balloon*
- *a clothespin*

1. Push one end of the
string through the straw.
(If it gets stuck, suck the
string through.)

2. Tie this end to a chair
leg.

3. Tape the other end of
the string near the ceiling
at the opposite end of a
large room.

4. Inflate the balloon,
twist its neck and clamp it
with the clothespin so that
no air escapes.

5. Use two pieces of tape
to attach the balloon to the
straw with the clothespin
pointing toward the chair
leg.

6. While holding the
neck of the balloon closed,
remove the clothespin.
Untwist the neck. Let the
balloon jet blast off.

was pushed forward. The same thing will happen if you stand on a skateboard holding a basket of apples. If you throw the basket forward you will be propelled backward on the skateboard.

How does it work?

When the inflated balloon was closed, there was equal air pressure against all the insides of the balloon. The balloon stayed still. When you removed the clothespin, the air pushed out of the back of the balloon and the balloon

What happens if . . .

● you inflate the balloon less?
● you use a larger balloon?
● your balloon travels straight across the room instead of at a slant?
● you insert a 5-cm (2-inch) piece of straw in the balloon's neck and tape it in place? Does the balloon travel as quickly or as far?

Porcupine Balloons

When a porcupine fish is in danger, it quickly fills itself up with water. It looks like a big, fierce balloon covered with spines. If it's caught and taken out of the water, it doubles its size with air instead of water. If it is put back into the water, it zooms away just like the jet in Balloon Blast-off.

Look Ma, No Hands

Can you pick up a glass of water without touching the glass?
Impossible? Not if you use this scientific trick.

You'll need:
○ **a wide-mouthed glass**
○ **water**
○ **a stretched balloon**

1. Half fill the glass with water.

2. Hold the balloon in the glass. Blow it up until it fills the glass and then some. Holding the balloon's mouth closed, lift the balloon and the glass up into the air. Ta da! You deserve a round of applause.

How does it work?

As you hold onto the balloon and lift, the air inside the glass has more room to spread out. It has less pressure than the air that is pushing against the bottom of the glass. In addition, the friction of the inflated balloon pushing against the glass stops the balloon from pulling out.

What happens if . . .
● you put more water in the glass?
● you use a tall narrow glass?

Waterglass Relay

After you've impressed your friends with your amazing skills, use the same trick to play a game with them.

You'll need:
- *2 bowls or pails filled with water*
- *2 identical empty pails*
- *2 identical balloons*
- *2 plastic glasses*
- *a metre (yard) stick*

1. Divide into two even teams and line up.

2. The leader of each team half fills a glass with water taken from the filled pail. She holds the balloon in the glass then blows it up until it fills the glass. Holding the balloon's mouth closed, she carries the glass of water to the empty pail that is 8 m (26 feet) away.

3. The leader deflates the balloon, pours her water into the empty pail, and runs back holding the glass and balloon in her hand.

She hands them to the second person and goes to the end of the line.

4. Each person does the same thing until one team is finished.

5. Measure the height of the water in the far pail. The winning team is the one with the most water.

If you don't have enough people for teams, you can simply have a waterglass race with a friend.

39

Which is Stronger —You or Air?

Challenge a friend to blow up a balloon that's inside a bottle. She'll probably think it's a snap. This experiment will change her mind.

You'll need:
- ○ *a balloon*
- ○ *an empty 750-mL (26-ounce) pop bottle*

1. Insert the balloon into the neck of the bottle.

2. Stretch the neck of the balloon back over the bottle's mouth.

3. Challenge your friend to blow into the balloon and inflate it inside the bottle. What does she think of her strength now?

How does it work?

When you blow into the balloon, the air in the bottle is compressed. This means that it is forced into a smaller space because the balloon takes up some of the space in the bottle. The compressed air is strong enough to push against the balloon and stop it from being inflated further.

When a lot of air is compressed into a small space and then released, it has a large amount of energy. This energy can power machines that make snow, spray paint cars and sand-blast the outside of buildings.

If compressed air is strong enough to do all this and more, no wonder your friend couldn't inflate the balloon.

What happens if . . .
● you use a larger bottle?
● you stretch the balloon before inserting it into the bottle?

Giant Balloon Sculptures

Instead of using clay or modelling clay such as Plasticine the next time you create a sculpture, try something a little different. How about making a sculpture out of 5000 balloons? That's how many balloons were used to build a giant red, white and blue airplane in Connecticut, U.S.A. If this sounds too ambitious, you can start with an 1800-balloon merry-go-round or a 1600-balloon tree. All of these were made by tying inflated balloons onto a metal frame of loosely woven wires. If you're not too sure how to go about making a balloon sculpture, there are lots of balloon artists in North America who can teach you how. Balloon artistry has been ballooning in the last few years.

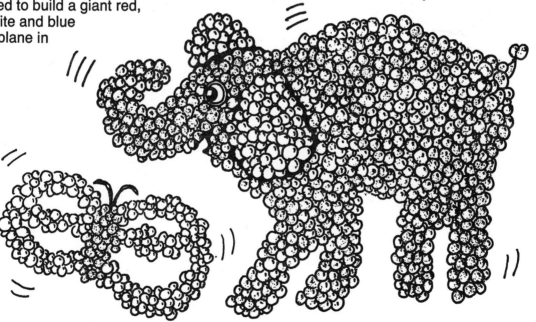

WATER WORKS

How can water flow uphill? Why do submarines sink? How can a boat float on land? Answer these and other puzzlers when you do the next six experiments.

An Underwater Diver

About 370 years ago a French scientist, René Descartes, invented a toy called an underwater diver. Here's how to make a modern version of his amazing diver. Why not make more than one and have a diving race with a friend?

You'll need:
- ○ *a plastic cap from a pen*
- ○ *a ball of Plasticine or other modelling clay the size of a marble*
- ○ *a balloon*
- ○ *scissors*
- ○ *an empty 1-L (1-quart) jar*
- ○ *water*
- ○ *a rubber band*

1. Cut off the clip or tail of the pen cap.

2. Roll the Plasticine into a worm shape and wrap it around the cap about 0.5 cm (¼ inch) from the opening. This is your diver.

3. Cut the balloon in half across its width.

4. Fill the jar with water to the brim.

5. Float the diver so that its top is at the surface of the water but not above it. You may have to adjust the amount of Plasticine slightly to get it just right.

6. Stretch the balloon so that it is taut over the mouth of the jar. Use the rubber band to hold it in place.

7. Press on the balloon and the diver descends. Stop pressing and what happens?

How does it work?

The diver floats near the surface because there is an air bubble trapped in its tip. When you press on the balloon, there is greater water pressure in the jar and on the diver. This presses on the air bubble, making it smaller. Since there isn't enough air to keep the diver afloat, it sinks to the bottom. When you remove your hand, there is less water pressure. The bubble enlarges to its original size and the diver ascends.

What happens if . . .
● the jar isn't full to the brim with water?
● you pull up on the balloon when the diver is at the bottom?

Balloons with Hard Shells
Air-filled tanks shaped like long balloons enable human divers to stay underwater for long periods of time. A metal scuba tank is strapped onto the back of the diver with a tube leading to his mouth for air. The air in the tank lasts anywhere between ten minutes and two hours depending on the experience of the diver and the temperature and depth of the water. The deeper a diver swims, the greater the water pressure on his lungs, and the more air he uses to keep his lungs filled with the normal amount of air.

45

Water Flowing Uphill

Do you think that you can make water flow uphill? It's not as impossible as it sounds with some simple science.

You'll need:

- O *a stretched balloon*
- O *a spool of thread with a single hole in the centre*
- O *a clothespin*
- O *a ball of Plasticine or other modelling clay the size of a small tomato*
- O *a pencil*
- O *53 cm (21 inches) of plastic tubing that is 0.5 cm (¼ inch) in diameter (you can buy it in an aquarium store)*
- O *a 1-L (1-quart) jar*
- O *water*
- O *a stick of chewing gum*

1. Stretch the neck of the balloon over one end of the spool.

2. Inflate the balloon by blowing through the other hole in the spool. Twist the neck of the balloon and hold it closed with the clothespin. Set this aside while you set up the next part.

3. Flatten the Plasticine to make a lid for the jar. Use a pencil to drill two holes 2 cm (¾ inch) apart through the lid.

4. Cut the tubing to make two pieces, one 21 cm (8 inches) long and the other 32 cm (13 inches).

5. Insert the tubes into the holes in the Plasticine so that each tube sticks up about 16 cm (6¼ inches) above the lid. Mould the Plasticine around both tubes so that there are no air holes.

6. Fill the jar two-thirds full of water.

46

7. Put the Plasticine lid on the jar tightly. The end of the longer tube should be deep in the water. The end of the shorter tube should be in the air above the water.

8. Push the other end of the shorter tube through the open hole in the spool until the tube reaches the neck of the balloon. If the tube doesn't fit in the hole snugly, use some chewing gum to plug up any small air spaces where the tube enters the spool.

9. Holding your jar in the kitchen sink remove the clothespin and untwist the neck of the balloon. Squeeze the balloon with both hands to force the balloon's air into the shorter tube. What happens with the longer tube?

Congratulations! You have just made water flow uphill.

How does it work?

When you push air into the jar by squeezing the balloon, you increase the air pressure on the water. The air pressing down on the water is strong enough to push the water up the longer tube and out into the air. Liquid soap dispensers and spray bottles work the same way.

What happens if . . .

● you blow air into the longer tube once the balloon is deflated?
● you suck air out of the shorter tube?

47

The Balloon-motor Boat Race

Have you ever dreamed of speeding across a lake in a motorboat race? If you can't afford a real motorboat, why not make a balloon-motor boat. In fact, make two kinds and see which one goes farther. May the best boat win.

You'll need:
- O *a 2-L (2-quart) milk carton*
- O *2 identical balloons*
- O *scissors*
- O *a bathtub of water*

1. Cut the carton in half lengthwise.

2. Cut a small hole in the middle of the flat end of one half-carton.

3. Cut an identical hole where the end meets the bottom in the other half-carton as shown.

4. Put the mouth of each balloon through each hole and inflate the balloons to the same size. Hold the balloons closed while you put the boats into the tub. On your mark, get set, let go! Which one goes farther? Why?

Inflating a Balloon Underwater

Water spiders live in underwater balloons. The balloons are spun out of silk thread and are filled with air bubbles. Where do the bubbles come from? The spider carries them down from the surface, one at a time between its hind legs, and puts them in the balloon. When the balloon is filled with air, the spider stays inside on the look-out for food. When it sees an insect, it darts out, catches it and brings it into the balloon to eat.

How does it work?

The balloon with its mouth in the water goes farther because the air leaves the balloon more slowly. The air inside the balloon lasts longer and can give the balloon thrust to move it forward for a longer time.

What happens if . . .

● you inflate the balloons less?
● you cut the holes bigger?
● you cut the holes smaller?

Q: What did the big balloon say to the small balloon?

A: I bet my pop is bigger than your pop.

Sink a Submarine

Have you ever wondered what makes a submarine sink? A submarine has large "ballast" tanks that run the length of the ship. When a submarine is on the surface of the water, these tanks are filled with air. When a submarine wants to sink, sea water is let into the tanks. How much water should a submarine take in to reach the bottom of the ocean?

You'll need:
- *water*
- *a bathtub*
- *5 small stretched balloons, all the same size*
- *Liquid Paper*

1. Fill the tub three-quarters full with cold water.

2. Inflate one balloon and tie it. Put it in the tub. What happens?

3. Put the mouth of the second balloon over the faucet of a sink. You may need an adult to help you with this next part. Pour water into the balloon until it is one-quarter the size of the first balloon. Holding the mouth of the balloon closed, carefully remove it from the faucet. Inflate the balloon so that it is the same size as the first one. Put it in the tub. What happens?

Waterballoon Toss

Try this game at your next summer picnic. Have your friends choose partners. You'll need one small water-filled balloon for every pair.

The pairs form a straight line. Each person faces his or her partner and takes one step backwards. You now have two lines of people about 60 cm (2 feet) apart. Give a balloon to each person in one of the lines. On the signal, the balloon holder tosses the balloon to his or her partner, who tries to catch it. The partners both take one step back and the balloon is tossed again. The game continues until there is one pair left with a whole balloon *and* dry clothes.

4. Pour water into two more balloons until one is one-half and the other is three-quarters the size of the first one. Blow them up to the same size as the original balloon. Put them in the water. What happens?

5. Pour water into the last balloon until it is as big as the first one. Put it in the tub.

6. You have a fleet of five submarines at different levels. With the Liquid Paper, mark the level of the tub water on the surface of the balloon. Lift each balloon straight out of the water. What do you notice about the level of the water inside the balloon?

How does it work?

The air inside the balloon keeps it afloat. The more air there is, the higher the balloon floats.

The more water there is in the ballast tanks of a submarine, the lower a submarine sinks. When it wants to rise to the surface, a submarine pumps compressed air into the ballast tanks. The air forces the water out.

What happens if . . .

● you puncture the balloons at the ends when you have finished the experiment?

Build a Hovercraft

Do you think taking a bath is boring?
How about making a hovercraft to liven things up?
Hovercraft are vehicles that travel over
water or land on a cushion of air. They carry
thousands of kilograms (pounds) of cargo.
Your hovercraft won't carry that much, but you'll
still have a blast using it.

You'll need:
- O *a nail*
- O *a plastic lid (from a margarine or yoghurt container)*
- O *a ball of Plasticine or other modelling clay the size of a meatball*
- O *a straw*
- O *a balloon*
- O *a friend*

1. Use the nail to puncture a hole in the middle of the plastic lid.

2. Roll the Plasticine into a cylinder with flat ends.

3. Starting in the middle of one end, drill a hole through the cylinder with the straw. Remove the straw.

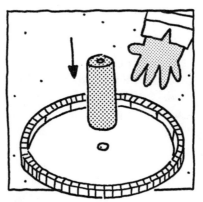

4. Place the hole in the cylinder over the hole in the lid.

5. Flatten the bottom edges of the Plasticine so that it sticks to the lid.

6. Inflate the balloon and hold it closed while a friend fits the neck over the other end of the Plasticine.

7. Set the hovercraft on the water and let go of the balloon. Bon voyage!

Balloons Help Fish Swim

Inside many fish there are balloons called swimbladders. Swimbladders filled with air, help the fish float. When a fish swims deeper, there is more water pressure on its swimbladder. The fish inflates its bladder to keep afloat. When it rises, there is less water pressure, and the swimbladder "burps" out some of its air.

How does it work?

Your hovercraft changes directions while moving over the surface of the water. This is because the air rushing out of the neck of the balloon comes out unevenly. First, it comes out on one side of the neck and makes bubbles under one part of the lid. This tilts the lid slightly and it moves in a direction opposite to the side with air bubbles. Then the air comes out of the other side of the neck and the hovercraft changes direction.

A Land Floater

A real hovercraft can go from water to land.
But you'd have a difficult time getting your bathtub
hovercraft (see page 52) to work out of water.
Try this land hovercraft instead.

You'll need:
- O *glue*
- O *an empty spool of thread with one hole through its centre*
- O *a record that no one wants anymore*
- O *a balloon*
- O *a clothespin*

1. Glue the spool to the middle of the record so that the holes line up with each other.

2. Inflate the balloon fully, twist its neck and clamp it with the clothespin so that no air escapes.

3. Stretch the neck of the balloon over the end of the spool.

4. Put the record on a very smooth surface. Remove the clothespin. How does this hovercraft compare with the water version on page 52?

How does it work?

The air from the balloon forms a thin air cushion between the record and the surface it is on. This air cushion eliminates most of the friction that usually stops an object from moving over a surface.

What happens if . . .
- you use a smaller record?
- you inflate the balloon less?

Balloons and Whales Don't Mix

Companies, community fairs and even schools sometimes release hundreds of helium filled balloons into the sky to celebrate special events. When these balloons lose their helium, they sometimes land in the ocean where they are eaten by whales and dolphins. Unfortunately, rather than just get indigestion, these sea mammals die. In order to prevent this, many people are using giant balloon sculptures instead of balloon releases. How about a life-size whale built out of balloons at your next celebration? You'll have a whale of a good time.

HELIUM AND HOT AIR HIGH JINKS

What's lighter than air but still is air?
You'll solve this puzzle and other mysteries when
you try these next experiments.

How to Stop a Blimp from Escaping

Blimps are those giant footballs you
sometimes see cruising in the sky. They usually
have the name of a company written on
their side. Blimps are filled with a gas called helium.
Helium is much lighter than air. In fact, it's the
second lightest gas known to man.
If helium is that light, why don't blimps float up
into space and disappear? Can you figure out
a way to stop a blimp from escaping?

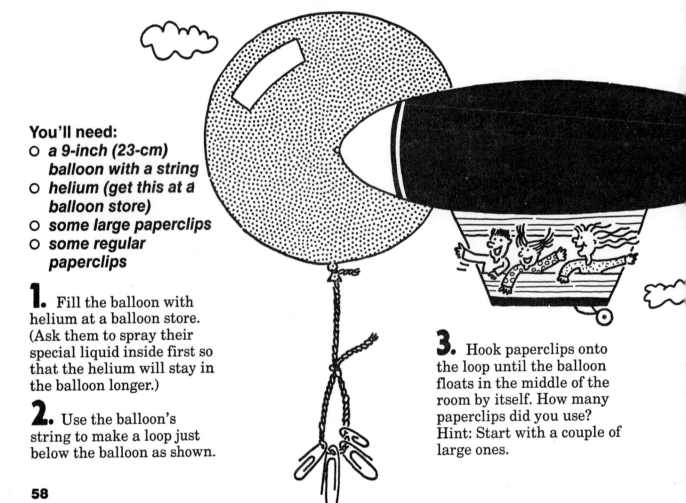

You'll need:
- ○ *a 9-inch (23-cm) balloon with a string*
- ○ *helium (get this at a balloon store)*
- ○ *some large paperclips*
- ○ *some regular paperclips*

1. Fill the balloon with helium at a balloon store. (Ask them to spray their special liquid inside first so that the helium will stay in the balloon longer.)

2. Use the balloon's string to make a loop just below the balloon as shown.

3. Hook paperclips onto the loop until the balloon floats in the middle of the room by itself. How many paperclips did you use? Hint: Start with a couple of large ones.

Flying Giant Trees

Logging companies use blimps to harvest giant trees that grow near mountaintops. First, a helicopter lowers a logging crew into the forest. After the trees are chopped down and cut into logs, an overhead blimp lowers a thick cable or rope into the forest. A logger makes a noose at the end of the cable and puts it around the log. The blimp lifts the log into the air and flies it to a waiting truck in a nearby valley. This kind of lumbering is called aerial logging. It may seem like a lot of work but it's less work (and less expensive) than building a road to reach the mountaintops.

How does it work?

Paperclips wouldn't be very effective as a weight on a real-life blimp. Besides, they'd look silly. Real blimps need three kinds of weight, or "ballast," to keep them at their usual travelling height of 330 m (1080 feet) above the earth's surface. The ballast consists of fuel, 11-kg (25-pound) bags of lead shot, and oh yes, passengers. Before deciding how much ballast to take up in the blimp, the pilot checks air temperature, barometric pressure and distance above sea level. These three measurements tell him how much lift the blimp has on that day. For example, if the barometer shows that the air pressure is high, the blimp will have less lift and so will need less ballast.

After you've stopped your blimp from escaping, remove the paperclips and make a Flouncer (next page).

Q: What did the balloon say when it drove into the gas station?

A: Fill me up.

A New Pet—The Flouncer

Have you always wanted a pet that is easy
to care for and fun to be with? Well, here's your chance.
Make a Flouncer and get ready for action.

You'll need:
- *1 roll of crêpe paper*
- *scissors*
- *glue*
- *1 sheet of plain bond paper*
- *felt-tip markers (the kind that write on plastic)*
- *tape*
- *a 9-inch (23-cm) helium-filled balloon that has been sprayed at a balloon store to keep the helium in longer*

1. Cut four strips of crêpe paper, each 60 cm (24 inches) long.

2. Glue the ends of two strips together to form a corner.

3. Fold the bottom strip over the top strip and crease.

4. Fold the other strip over and crease.

5. Continue to fold the strips alternately until you have a small square.

6. Glue the ends together. When you open it up, you will have a loosely braided leg for your Flouncer.

7. Make a second leg with the other two strips.

8. Fold the bond paper in half. On one side draw a large shoe print at least 15 cm (6 inches) long. Keeping the paper folded, cut out the shoe print. You now have two shoes.

9. Glue each shoe to one end of each leg.

10 Tape the legs near the bottom of the balloon and let go. Your Flouncer should stand up with its feet on the floor. If the feet float above the floor, add a crêpe paper tail for more weight.

11 Use the markers to draw a face on the balloon.

12 Your Flouncer is now ready for action. Its favourite trick is the "Sideways Shuffle." Move one leg to the side and the other will follow. Try throwing it up in the air. How about taking it for a walk down stairs?

Your Flouncer won't work well on rugs or carpeted stairs—it just drags its feet.

Q: What do you call a noisy balloon party?

A: A hullaballoon.

Warm Air vs. Cold Air

Do you need a way to stump a know-it-all? Ask him which takes up less space, warm air or cold air? When he doesn't know the answer, you can show him how you became the air expert.

You'll need:
- *a balloon*
- *a measuring tape*
- *a refrigerator*

1. Inflate the balloon and tie it tightly.

2. Measure the balloon around its widest part. Mark the balloon where you measured it.

3. Put the balloon in the freezer overnight.

4. Measure it around its widest part. Which is bigger: the warm or cool balloon?

? How does it work?

Air is made up of tiny invisible particles called molecules. When air is cold, the molecules move closer together. That's why cold air takes up less space, or "contracts." When the cold air in the balloon contracted, the balloon got smaller. Would bicycle tires need slightly more air in cooler weather?

What happens if . . .

● you leave the balloon in the freezer longer?
● you hold the balloon under hot water for a few minutes?
● you fill the balloon with water and do the same experiment?

The First Rubber Balloon

The first rubber balloon was made by an English scientist, Michael Faraday, in 1824. He cut two round sheets of rubber and glued their edges together.

It wasn't until 1847 that balloons were made on a mould as they are today. Moulded balloons were made by hand one at a time. Today they are made by machine.

Losing Elasticity

Elasticity is how much a thing can stretch.

Stretch a deflated balloon as far as you can. Measure and record its length. Put an identical balloon in the fridge overnight. Stretch and measure it. Does cold affect the elasticity of a balloon?

The cold balloon doesn't stretch as far because rubber becomes brittle or stiff when it is cold. It loses its elasticity. What happens if you leave the balloon in the freezer for two days?

Get a Rise out of Air

Which is lighter, hot air or cold air? Try this experiment to help you find out, and you'll also discover how hot air balloons rise into the sky.

You'll need:
- *2 large identical balloons*
- *scissors*
- *2 straight pins*
- *1 straw*
- *1 piece of yarn 30 cm (1 foot) long*
- *1 candle in a candleholder*

1. Cut both balloons in half widthwise and discard the neck part.

2. Stick a pin into the centre of the rounded part of one balloon. Then stick the pin through the straw 1 cm (¼ inch) from its end.

3. Attach the other balloon to the other end of the straw in the same way.

4. Pull the sides of the balloons apart so that they don't stick together.

5. Tie one end of the yarn near the middle of the straw. Tie the other end to a place where the straw can hang freely.

6. Move the yarn slowly along the straw until the two balloons balance.

7. Important: Do this part with an adult. Light the candle. Hold the candle about 12 cm (5 inches) underneath the opening of one balloon. What happens?

How does it work?

The candle flame warmed up the air inside the balloon. When air is heated, its molecules move farther apart. Since there is more space between the molecules, the hot air is lighter. The heated balloon rises because its air is lighter than the cooler air in the other balloon.

Hot air balloons use this principle to rise into the air. Attached to the bottom of the nylon balloon is a basket or gondola which carries a propane gas burner. The flame from this burner heats the air inside the balloon which is open at the bottom. To bring the balloon down, the air inside is allowed to cool.

Some balloonists fill their balloons with helium instead of hot air. Since this gas is much lighter than air, the basket or gondola attached to the balloon carries weights. The weights are usually bags filled with sand. By throwing sandbags overboard, the balloonist controls the height that the balloon rises.

A Hot Air Balloon Record

People are always trying to set records. Balloonists are no different. In 1987, two men set a world record for crossing the Atlantic Ocean in a hot air balloon. They started out from Maine, U.S.A. and landed in Northern Ireland. The balloon used on this flight was as tall as a 21-storey building. Can you imagine the excitement in Ireland as people there watched a balloon the size of an apartment building descend from the sky?

Q: What did the balloon say when it caught its friend fibbing?

A: You're full of hot air.

Create a Vacuum

Next time you're using a vacuum cleaner feel the suction at the end of the hose. You will astound your friends when you show them how you can create a similar suction using only a balloon, a bottle and water.

You'll need:
- *a stretched balloon*
- *an empty 750-mL (26-ounce) pop bottle*
- *tap water*

1. Place the neck of the balloon over the mouth of the bottle.

2. Hold the lower half of the bottle under running hot water for a few minutes. What happens?

3. Now hold the bottle under running cold water until the balloon is sucked into the bottle. Why did this happen?

How does it work?

The hot water heated the air in the bottle. Hot air molecules move farther apart, or "expand," and take up more room than cold air molecules. The hot air pushed into the balloon and inflated it. As you know from the Warm Air vs. Cold Air experiment on page 62, cold air contracts. When the cold air contracted, it left a space in the bottle with no air in it. This empty space is called a vacuum. The balloon was pushed into this vacuum by the greater pressure outside the bottle.

Vacuum cleaners have a fan that pushes air out the back of the machine. This creates a partial vacuum in the hose. The air around the nozzle rushes in carrying dirt with it.

Canned food stays fresh for two years because it is vacuum packed. The food-filled can is heated to 132°C (270°F) and then cooled. This process seals the can so that no air can enter and cause the food to spoil.

What happens if . . .

- you use a larger bottle?
- you cool the bottle in the freezer instead of with cold water?

Up, Up and Away

If you're looking for an unusual birthday gift for a friend, why not treat her to a ride in a hot air balloon? The only drawback is that it costs about $150. Hot air balloons come in all shapes and sizes. If your friend sees a floating dinosaur, truck, house or even a flying saucer with little green men while she's up in the air, you'll know she's not just full of hot air. Companies use these balloons to advertise their names and people celebrate their birthdays and anniversaries in them.

Sports enthusiasts use hot air balloons in competitions. One of the most popular ballooning events is a hare and hounds race. One balloon (the hare) takes off and the others (the hounds) try to follow it. The hounds must land as close to the hare as possible. This is not as easy as it sounds. While balloonists can control their rising and falling by changing the air temperature inside the balloon, they depend on the whim of the winds to carry them any distance. No wonder hot air ballooning has never become an Olympic event.

CHARGE IT

Why not enter your cereal in the Olympics or create lightning in your room or . . . . Read on. You'll get a charge out of the balloon tricks in this next section.

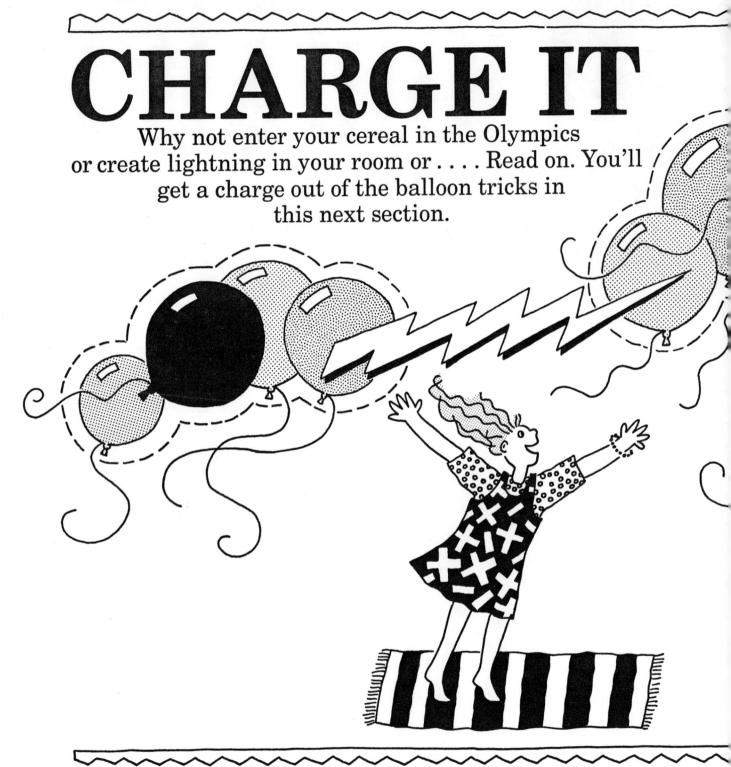

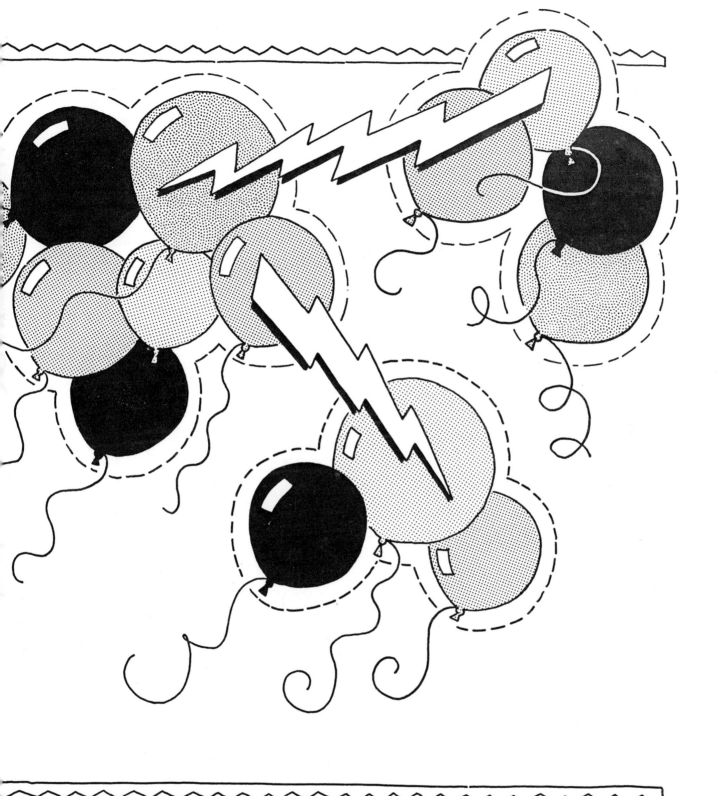

Angry Balloons

When two people are angry, they often want nothing to do with each other. Balloons are the same. In this case, it's static electricity rather than words that causes them to stay apart.

You'll need:
- O *2 identical balloons*
- O *tape*
- O *clean, dry hair*

1. Inflate the balloons to the same size and tie them.

2. Stick a piece of tape onto the neck of each balloon. Tape the balloons to the edge of a table so that they are hanging side by side with no space between them.

3. While you hold the balloons still, put your head between them. Rub your hair on both balloons by shaking your head as if you're saying "no." This creates static electricity.

4. Move back and let go of the balloons. What happens?

How does it work?

All things are made of tiny molecules that are made up of invisible atoms. On the outside of each atom are particles of electricity called electrons. Electrons like to be evenly

spread out or balanced like people on a see-saw. Sometimes the electrons jump off. When you rub a balloon on your hair, some electrons jump from your hair onto the balloon. The balloon now has extra electrons on the rubbed side. When something has extra electrons, we say it has a negative $(-)$ electrical charge. Since you rubbed both balloons on your hair, they both got a negative $(-)$ charge. When things have the same kind of charge, they move away from, or "repel," each other.

What happens if . . .
● you put your hand between the balloons after you've given them a negative charge?
● you put your hand beside one of the balloons after you've given them a negative charge?

Q: What did one angry balloon say to the other balloon?

A: You rub me the wrong way.

Snap, Crackle and Hop

You've heard of Mexican jumping beans.
How about jumping cereals? Run an Olympic
jumping event for puffed cereals using
some basic electricity principles. Which one
will be the winner?

You'll need:
- ○ *3 saucers*
- ○ *3 kinds of puffed cereals like Cheerios, Rice Crispies and puffed wheat or corn*
- ○ *3 identical balloons*
- ○ *clean, dry hair*

1. Put a small handful of each cereal into its own saucer.

2. Inflate and tie the balloons.

3. Use a separate balloon for each saucer. Rub a balloon back and forth on your hair a dozen times. Hold the now charged part of the balloon near one of the cereals. How easily are the puffs attracted? How many stick to the balloon?

4. Do the same with the other two balloons and cereals. How do they compare with the first cereal? Does the size of the cereal pieces make a difference?

How does it work?

When you rub the balloon on your hair, the balloon becomes negatively (−) charged. The cereal is neutral or has no charge. The negative (−) charge on the balloon repels or pushes the electrons in the puffs to the opposite side. This leaves a positive (+) charge on the side nearest the balloon. Since opposite charges attract each other, the puffs are attracted to the balloon. The air holes inside the puffs make them light enough to be lifted by the static electricity.

What happens if:

● you rub the balloons on your hair longer?
● you mix the cereals together?
● you try the experiment again during wet weather?
● you bring another charged balloon near a balloon with puffs on it?
● you use cereal that is flaked rather than puffed?

1, 2, 3 . . . GO!

Wet Weather Spoilsport

The best time to do experiments with static electricity is on a cold, dry day. In warm weather, when the air is damp, electrical charges are attracted to the air. If you try to charge an object on a wet day, the electrons go into the air instead of gathering on the object that you want to charge.

Lightning Without a Rainstorm

A lightning bolt across the sky can be
both frightening and fascinating. You can create
lightning indoors without a thunderstorm.
In fact, it will work best on a dry day in winter.
Why not invite some friends to give you a hand?
They might get a charge out of it.

You'll need:
- *an inflated balloon for each person*
- *a dark room*

1. In a dark room, rub the balloon vigorously on a wool sweater or on your hair.

2. Hold your finger near the balloon. What happens? If several people are trying this, can you arrange a series of flashes so that one streak of lightning seems to be travelling across the room?

How does it work?

When you rubbed the balloon, it received a negative electric charge. The extra electrons on the balloon were attracted to your neutral finger. When they jumped from the balloon to your finger, you saw a spark.

Lightning works in a similar way. Thunderstorm clouds are heavily charged with static electricity. They carry positive charges at the top and negative charges near the bottom. The negative charges zap downwards toward the earth and form a tunnel. The positive charges on the ground are attracted to these negative charges, and rush up the tunnel to meet them. That's when you see a flash of lightning in the sky. If the electricity from a single flash could be harnessed, you'd have enough to power your house for three months.

The Guinness Balancing Challenge

This balloon-balancing trick won't get you into *The Guinness Book of World Records* because it involves some cheating, but it will fool your friends. Have a contest to see who can balance a balloon on his or her head the longest. You'll hold the record every time if you secretly rub the balloon on your hair before you start.

Q: When is a balloon like a bull?

A: When it charges.

75

A Magnetic Balloon

Challenge a friend to move a tin can across
a floor without touching the can. She might try blowing on
it, but you can show her how easy it is when you
use a magnetic balloon.

Balloon Power!

You'll need:
- *a clean, empty juice can*
- *an inflated balloon*

1. Remove the label and the two ends from the juice can.

2. Lay the can on a smooth surface (a wooden floor will do) with the seam facing upward.

3. Put a negative charge on the balloon by rubbing it on clean, dry hair or wool.

4. Hold the charged part of the balloon near the can and move the balloon over the can to start it rolling.

5. Once the can is rolling, recharge the balloon and try to make it roll in the opposite direction.

How does it work?

The negatively charged balloon attracted the can. The pull on the can is strong enough to overcome the friction that holds it in place. Once the can is rolling, it needs very little electrical pull to continue on the smooth surface. It's amazing that the charge on the balloon is able to stop the can and force it to reverse its direction.

What happens if . . .
● you use a smaller can?
● you use a magnet instead of a balloon?

Zap and Pull Race

Here's a game to try with some friends and your "magnetic balloon." Give an inflated balloon and an empty tin can to each contestant. Line the cans up at one end of a room or hall with a smooth floor. On the signal, everyone charges their balloons on their hair. The first person to pull his can to the far side of the room using only the charged balloon is the winner. Recharging the balloon is allowed. (Hint: the cleaner the hair, the stronger the charge.)

An Electric Tug-of-War

This game is for two people. But if the room is large enough, several pairs can play at the same time.

Lay an empty tin can in the centre of a smooth floor. The opponents kneel on opposite sides of the can. Each person must use a charged balloon to pull the can to their end of the room.

No one is a winner until the can touches the wall. So move quickly and keep rubbing your hair. You never know who will win the Electric Tug-of-War.

An Unusual Flashlight

If you ever have a power failure at night,
you can be the first in your family to shed some
light on the problem.

You'll need:
- *a balloon*
- *a fluorescent tube or small neon bulb*
- *clean, dry hair*

1. Inflate and tie the balloon.

2. In a dark room, put a charge on the balloon by rubbing it on your hair.

3. Immediately touch the metal prongs at the end of the fluorescent tube to the charged area of the balloon. Move the prongs all over the charged surface. What happens?

How does it work?

The electrical charge on the balloon makes the tiny atoms of mercury inside the tube jump around. When the atoms are warmed up (like you are, after exercise), they give off an invisible light called ultra-violet light. The inside of the tube is coated with a white powder called phosphor. When the ultra-violet light hits the powder, it glows. This glow is the light we see.

Static electricity is used in photocopying machines. Let's say you wanted to make copies of a birthday party invitation to send to all your friends. When you put your invitation into a copying machine, a light shines onto the paper. The picture casts shadows onto a negatively charged drum. A positively charged ink powder is attracted to the drum. When negatively charged blank paper passes over the drum, the ink powder jumps onto it. The powder is baked onto the paper so it will stay permanently. Run your fingers over a sheet from a copier. Can you feel the raised letters? Can you feel how warm it is?

What happens if . . .
● you touch the balloon to the side of the tube?
● you rub the balloon with wool or nylon or fur?

A Hair Raising Experience
Ghost stories can make your hair stand on end. A balloon can do the same for you in just a few seconds.

Put a negative charge on a balloon by rubbing it on your hair. When you hold the balloon slightly away from your head, strands of hair stand on end. These strands became positively charged when they lost some electrons during rubbing. Since opposite charges attract, the hair was attracted to the balloon.

No Strings Attached

Puppeteers move marionettes with strings.
You can get one jump ahead of them. You can make
paper marionettes walk and dance with invisible
strings called static electricity.

You'll need:
- O *a sheet of paper*
- O *scissors*
- O *a balloon*
- O *clean, dry hair*

1. Cut out several paper people that are 3 cm (1 inch) tall.

2. Inflate and tie the balloon.

3. Rub the balloon on your hair.

4. Put the rubbed surface of the balloon near the people. Can you make them stand? Why do some of them jump up and then back down?

How does it work?

The neutral paper puppets were attracted by the negatively charged balloon. When they touched the balloon, they became negatively charged too. Since like charges repel, the paper jumped away. After a few seconds, the puppets lost their negative charge to the air and were again attracted to the balloon.

What happens if . . .

● you use larger paper puppets?
● you use other kinds of paper like tissue paper, waxed paper, cardboard, Kleenex, or aluminum foil?
● you rub the balloon longer?
● you touch the figures with the other side of the balloon?

Can You Bend Water?

Put a charge on a balloon by rubbing it on your hair. Hold it near a thin stream of water. Voilà! You've bent water without touching it. The negative charge on the balloon attracted the neutral water.

A Magical Merry-go-round

Your friends will think you have magical
powers when you tell them that you can turn a
merry-go-round without touching it.
Sound impossible? Not really, if you use a
little static know-how.

You'll need:
- O *a sheet of paper*
- O *a ruler*
- O *scissors*
- O *a pencil*
- O *a sewing needle*
- O *thread*
- O *a cork*
- O *an inflated balloon*

1. Cut out a 5-cm (2-inch)
square piece of paper.

2. Fold the paper in half
and in half again to make a
small square. Make your
creases sharp.

3. Open up the square.
At each outer corner, draw
a square that is 2 cm (¾
inch) square. Cut out each
square and save it for the
next step. You now have a
cross with creases in it.

4. Lay the four small squares on top of one another. Draw a horse on the top square. Cut the horse out, cutting through all four squares. You now have four identical horses.

5. Attach a horse near the end of each arm of the cross by pulling a threaded needle through the horse and cross, remove the needle, and tie the thread to make a small loop.

6. Push the eye of the needle into the centre of the top of the cork so that the needle stands upright.

7. Balance the merry-go-round on the point of the needle where the two creases cross. The very tip of the needle can poke through the paper.

8. Rub the balloon on clean, dry hair. Hold the balloon near the merry-go-round and make circles in the air above it. What happens?

 How does it work?

When you rub the balloon on your hair, the balloon gains a negative charge. The paper arms of the cross are neutral. When you hold the balloon near an arm, the electrons at the end of the arm are repelled by the balloon's charge, and run to the other end of the arm. The end closest to the balloon now has a positive charge. Since opposite charges attract each other, the end of the arm is attracted to the balloon and follows it wherever it goes, even in circles.

Q: What do you get when you cross a sheep with a loon?

A: A ba-loon.

BE A CARBON DIOXIDE DETECTIVE

When people and animals breathe out, they exhale a gas called carbon dioxide. If you're a good detective, you can find carbon dioxide in your home and at school. Here are a few experiments to help you in your search.

Get the Inside Story

Have you ever passed by a fire extinguisher
and wondered what's inside it? You don't need to pull
one apart to find out. Just ask a friend
to help you with this experiment.

You'll need:
- O *a funnel or paper to make one*
- O *30 mL (2 Tbsp) baking soda*
- O *an empty 750-mL (26-ounce) pop bottle*
- O *a stretched balloon*
- O *50 mL (¼ cup) vinegar*

1. Use the funnel to put the baking soda into the bottle.

2. Have your friend ready with the stretched balloon. Pour the vinegar into the bottle. Ask your friend to quickly put the mouth of the balloon over the mouth of the bottle. Swish the liquid around until it stops foaming.

How does it work?

Why did the balloon blow up? It was filled with carbon dioxide. Carbon dioxide is produced when baking soda (bicarbonate of soda) and vinegar (an acid) mix together.

Some fire extinguishers are filled with pure carbon dioxide. They're used on ships, in garages and machine shops to put out engine and grease fires.

What happens if . . .
● you use more or less baking soda?
● you use more or less vinegar?
● you don't swish the liquid around?

The Baking Powder Challenge

Baking soda is sometimes used in cake recipes. So is baking powder. Bakeries prefer baking powder. Can you figure out why?

You'll need:
- *a funnel*
- *30 mL (2 Tbsp) baking soda*
- *30 mL (2 Tbsp) baking powder*
- *2 empty 750-mL (26-ounce) pop bottles*
- *vinegar*
- *2 stretched balloons*

1. Label one pop bottle baking soda and the other baking powder.

2. Follow the instuctions in the Get the Inside Story experiment on page 86. Use baking soda in one pop bottle and baking powder in the other. Which gives off more carbon dioxide?

How does it work?

The baking powder not only inflates balloons more, it also helps cakes rise higher. When you mix acids like fruit juices or milk powder with baking powder, carbon dioxide is produced. During baking, the heat expands tiny bubbles of carbon dioxide. This makes the cake rise.

What happens if . . .
- you change the amount of vinegar?
- you change the amounts of baking soda and baking powder?
- you use a smaller bottle?

Q: Why did the balloon keep burping?

A: It had a lot of gas.

The Pop Contest

Have you had any pop today? If so,
you've been drinking carbon dioxide. Don't worry.
There's water, sugar and flavouring mixed in
with it too. Some pops have more carbon dioxide
than others. Can you figure out which
pop has the most?

You'll need:

- *3 unopened 750-mL (26-ounce) bottles of club soda, cola, and carbonated orange drink*
- *3 identical stretched balloons*
- *a kitchen towel*

1. Open each bottle and immediately put the mouth of a balloon over the mouth of the bottle.

2. Put the bottoms of the bottles on a folded kitchen towel. Jiggle them back and forth for seven minutes. Get a friend to jiggle the third bottle.

How does it work?

When you jiggle each bottle, carbon dioxide bubbles are released and float to the surface of the water. They burst and go into the balloon. There is enough carbon dioxide to inflate the balloon. Which balloon inflated the most? Which pop has the most carbon dioxide?

What happens if . . .
● you jiggle the bottles longer than seven minutes?
● you try the same experiment with other soda pops? Make sure the bottles are the same size, and that you jiggle for the same length of time. Can you rank them in order from the highest to the lowest amount of carbon dioxide?

Try This Challenge
How much can you blow up an ordinary balloon using club soda and jiggling? Measure it around its widest part. Can you beat my record? My balloon inflated to 44 cm (17 inches) around.

Eating Carbon Dioxide

If it weren't for carbon dioxide, many of the foods you eat would be pretty flat. Cakes and cookies wouldn't rise and bread would look like crackers. Where's the carbon dioxide? Try this simple batter recipe and find out.

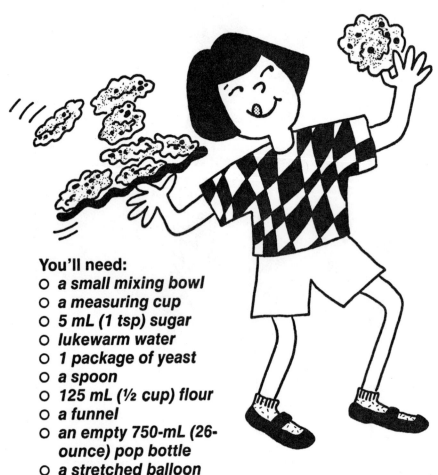

You'll need:
- a small mixing bowl
- a measuring cup
- 5 mL (1 tsp) sugar
- lukewarm water
- 1 package of yeast
- a spoon
- 125 mL (½ cup) flour
- a funnel
- an empty 750-mL (26-ounce) pop bottle
- a stretched balloon
- a crayon

1. In the bowl, mix the sugar with 75 mL (¼ cup) water.

2. Sprinkle the yeast on top and stir well.

3. Add 125 mL (½ cup) water and the flour. Mix well.

4. Use the funnel to pour this mixture into the pop bottle. Put the balloon over its mouth and place the bottle in a very warm place. With a crayon, mark a line on the bottle to show how high the mixture is.

5. After half an hour, what changes do you see?

- you change the amounts of the ingredients?
- you use other foods instead of flour? Be sure to use the same measurements. Will they produce the same amount of carbon dioxide? Will the length of time vary?

How does it work?

The yeast made the mixture rise in the bottle just like it helps bread dough rise before and during baking. When yeast grows, it gives off carbon dioxide. Some of it entered the balloon and inflated it. Most of the carbon dioxide remained in the mixture in the form of hundreds of tiny bubbles. When bread is baking, the bubbles push on the dough and cause it to rise. Air holes are formed throughout the bread. The carbon dioxide escapes through the air holes at the top of the bread and you are left with bread that is light and tasty to eat. Without yeast, bread would taste like paste. And who wants to eat that for lunch?

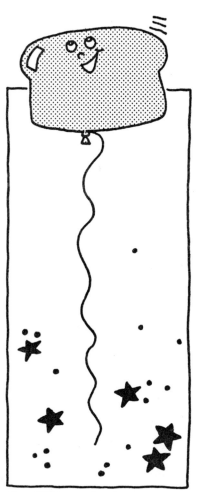

Q: When is a balloon like bread dough?

A: When it rises.

What Comes First?

Can you guess what balloons are made of? Stretch a balloon and let go. What happens? Now stretch a rubber band and let go. That's right. They both bounce back. That's because they are both made out of rubber, one of the very few materials in the world with a memory. No matter how many times you stretch rubber, it comes back to its original position.

Balloon manufacturers get their rubber from rubber trees. These 20-m (65-feet) tall trees grow near the equator in Malaysia and Indonesia.

Farmers in these countries tap rubber trees just like people in Canada tap maple trees for maple sap. But instead of drilling a hole in the tree, they make a long narrow cut in the bark. This cut runs all the way around the trunk on a slant. A white liquid called latex oozes out of the bottom of the cut. It drips into a cup that is attached to the tree.

The latex is poured into large containers. They are sent all over the world to factories that produce tires, rainboots, erasers, golf balls, running shoes, gloves, fire hoses and, of course, balloons.

Q: What does a balloon have for breakfast?

A: Air.

Q: What does a balloon have for lunch?

A: Air.

Q: What does a balloon have for supper?

A: Pop!

THE END OF THE BEGINNING

This is almost the end of the book, but it's really just the beginning. You can begin to design your own balloon experiments. You can also find out how the balloons you've been using are made.

Latex

Coagulant

The Birth of a Balloon

1. When liquid latex arrives at the factory, it is mixed with a colour and chemicals in a huge tank.

2. Aluminum moulds, which give a balloon its shape, are cleaned and dried.

3. There are hundreds of moulds attached to one tray. They are dipped into a tank and coated with a coagulant, a solution that helps keep the latex on the moulds.

Latex

Water & Chlorine

OUR HERO!

4. When the coagulant becomes sticky, the moulds are dipped into a tank of coloured latex. The latex sticks to the moulds.

5. A series of brushes sweeps by the moulds and forms a roll at the mouth of the balloons.

6. The latex-covered moulds are submerged in vats of water and chlorine. The coagulant is extracted from the inside of the balloon.

7. The balloons are baked in a large oven for half an hour. The heat turns the latex into solid rubber.

8. The balloons are removed from the moulds with bursts of air pressure from a narrow nozzle called an air hose. Once the balloons are rinsed clean, they are ready for packaging.

INDEX

A

Acids 87
Air 12, 13, 18–23, 26, 30, 32, 33, 37, 38, 40, 50, 51, 53, 55
Air bubbles 45, 49, 53
Air cushion 35, 52, 54
Airplanes 18, 19, 24, 25, 41
Air pressure 15, 17–19, 21, 23–25, 31, 33, 37, 38, 47, 59, 67
Atmosphere 23, 67
Atoms 71, 79

B

Baking powder 87
Baking soda 86, 87
Balance 12–13, 64
Ballast 50, 59
Balloonists 61, 65
Bernoulli, Daniel 18, 21
Blimps 58, 59
Boats
    Hovercraft 34, 35, 52–54
    Submarines 42, 50, 51
    Balloon-motorboat 48
Breathing 16, 17, 27, 84
Bugs
    Assassin 19

C

Carbon dioxide 85–91
Charge, electrical 68, 71–79, 81, 83
Coagulant 94, 95
Cold air 15, 62–64
Colour 15, 94
Compressed air 31, 41, 51
Contracting air 15, 63, 66

D

Descartes, René 44

Diaphragm 17
Dolphins 55

E

Ears 24, 25
Elasticity 63
Electrons 71, 73, 75, 79, 83
Elevator 25
Energy 41
Expanding air 66, 87

F

Fire extinguisher 86
Fish
    Porcupine 37
    Swimbladders 53
Fluorescent light 78, 79
Friction 38, 54, 77

G

Games 17, 21, 39, 51, 77
Gas 19, 23, 58, 65, 84

H

Heat 15, 27
Helicopter 59
Helium 55, 56, 58, 60, 65, 67
Hot air 64-66
Hot air balloons 61, 65
Hovercraft 28, 34, 52–54

L

Latex 92–95
Lift 18, 19, 59
Lightning 68, 74, 75
Lungs 16–18, 45

M

Machines 31, 41, 67, 79
Making balloons 63, 92–95
Marionettes 80

Molecules
    Air 63, 65, 67
    Rubber 26, 27

R

Riddles 9, 13, 19, 25, 27, 31, 35, 59, 65, 67, 71, 75, 83, 87
Rubber 15, 26, 33, 35, 63, 92

S

Scientists
    Bernoulli, Daniel 18, 21
    Descartes, René 44
Scuba tanks 45
Sculptures 41, 55
Spider
    water spider 49
Static electricity 70–73, 75, 79, 80
Submarines 42, 50, 51
Suction 32, 33, 66

T

Temperature 27, 45, 59, 61

V

Vacuum 24, 25, 66, 67

W

Water 14, 34, 37–39, 44–53, 81,
Water pressure 45, 53
Weather 23, 73
Weight 12, 13, 34, 35, 59, 61, 65
Whales 55

Y

Yeast 90, 91